THE
LITTLE BOOK OF
SELF-CARE
FOR
AQUARIUS

*Simple Ways to Refresh
and Restore—According
to the Stars*

CONSTANCE STELLAS

ADAMS MEDIA

NEW YORK LONDON TORONTO SYDNEY NEW DELHI

Adams Media
An Imprint of Simon & Schuster, Inc.
57 Littlefield Street
Avon, Massachusetts 02322

Copyright © 2019 by Simon & Schuster, Inc.

First Adams Media hardcover edition January 2019

ADAMS MEDIA and colophon are trademarks of Simon & Schuster.

For information about special discounts for bulk purchases,
please contact Simon & Schuster Special Sales at 1-866-506-1949 or
business@simonandschuster.com.

The Simon & Schuster Speakers Bureau can bring authors to your live event. For
more information or to book an event contact the Simon & Schuster Speakers
Bureau at 1-866-248-3049 or visit our website at www.simonspeakers.com.

Interior design by Colleen Cunningham
Interior images © Getty Images; Clipart.com

Manufactured in the United States of America

10 9 8 7 6 5 4 3 2

Library of Congress Cataloging-in-Publication Data has been applied for.

ISBN 978-1-5072-0984-4
ISBN 978-1-5072-0985-1 (ebook)

Dedication

To my ingenious, future-headed friends and clients,
with appreciation.

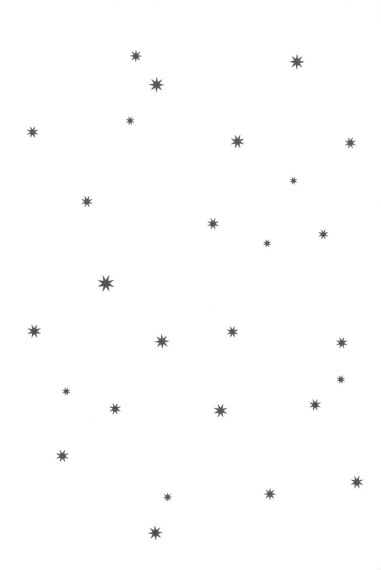

CONTENTS

Acknowledgments

I would like to thank Karen Cooper and everyone at Adams Media who helped with this book. To Brendan O'Neill, Katie Corcoran Lytle, Sarah Doughty, Eileen Mullan, Casey Ebert, Sylvia Davis, and everyone else who worked on the manuscripts. To Frank Rivera, Colleen Cunningham, and Katrina Machado for their work on the book's cover and interior design. I appreciated your team spirit and eagerness to dive into the riches of astrology.

Introduction

It's time for you to have a little *"me" time*—powered by the zodiac. By tapping into your Sun sign's astrological and elemental energies, *The Little Book of Self-Care for Aquarius* brings star-powered strength and cosmic relief to your life with self-care guidance tailored specifically for you.

You are blessed with a unique personality, Aquarius, and this book focuses on your true self. This book provides information on how to incorporate self-care into your life while teaching you just how important astrology is to your overall self-care routine. You'll learn more about yourself as you learn about your sign and its governing element, air. Then you can relax, rejuvenate, and stay balanced with more than one hundred self-care ideas and activities perfect for your Aquarius personality.

From trying acupuncture to joining an exotic food club, you will find plenty of ways to heal your mind, body, and active spirit. Now, let the stars be your self-care guide!

PART 1

SIGNS,
ELEMENTS,
AND
SELF-CARE

CHAPTER 1
WHAT IS SELF-CARE?

Astrology gives insights into whom to love, when to charge forward into new beginnings, and how to succeed in whatever you put your mind to. When paired with self-care, astrology can also help you relax and reclaim that part of yourself that tends to get lost in the bustle of the day. In this chapter you'll learn what self-care is—for you. (No matter your sign, self-care is more than just lit candles and quiet reflection, though these activities may certainly help you find the renewal that you seek.) You'll also learn how making a priority of personalized self-care activities can benefit you in ways you may not even have thought of. Whether you're a Leo, a Pisces, or a Taurus, you deserve rejuvenation and renewal that's customized to your sign—this chapter reveals where to begin.

What Self-Care Is

Self-care is any activity that you do to take care of yourself. It rejuvenates your body, refreshes your mind, or realigns your spirit. It relaxes and refuels you. It gets you ready for a new day or a fresh start. It's the practices, rituals, and meaningful activities that you do, just for you, that help you feel safe, grounded, happy, and fulfilled.

The activities that qualify as self-care are amazingly unique and personalized to who you are, what you like, and, in large part, what your astrological sign is. If you're asking questions about what self-care practices are best for those ruled by air and born under the unique eye of Aquarius, you'll find answers—and restoration—in Part 2. But, no matter which of those self-care activities speak to you and your unique place in the universe on any given day, it will fall into one of the following self-care categories—each of which pertains to a different aspect of your life:

* Physical self-care
* Emotional self-care
* Social self-care
* Mental self-care
* Spiritual self-care
* Practical self-care

When you practice all of these unique types of self-care—and prioritize your practice to ensure you are choosing the best options for your unique sign and governing element—know that you are actively working to create the version of yourself that the universe intends you to be.

Physical Self-Care

When you practice physical self-care, you make the decision to look after and restore the one physical body that has been bestowed upon you. Care for it. Use it in the best way you can imagine, for that is what the universe wishes you to do. You can't light the world on fire or move mountains if you're not doing everything you can to take care of your physical health.

Emotional Self-Care

Emotional self-care is when you take the time to acknowledge and care for your inner self, your emotional well-being. Whether you're angry or frustrated, happy or joyful, or somewhere in between, emotional self-care happens when you choose to sit with your emotions: when you step away from the noise of daily life that often drowns out or tamps down your authentic self. Emotional self-care lets you see your inner you as the cosmos intend. Once you identify your true emotions, you can either accept them and continue to move forward on your journey or you can try to change any negative emotions for the better. The more you acknowledge your feelings and practice emotional self-care, the more you'll feel the positivity that the universe and your life holds for you.

Social Self-Care

You practice social self-care when you nurture your relationships with others, be they friends, coworkers, or family members. In today's hectic world it's easy to let relationships fall to the wayside, but it's so important to share your life with others—and let others share their lives with you. Social self-care is reciprocal and often karmic. The support and love that you put out into the universe through social self-care is given back to you by those you socialize with—often tenfold.

Mental Self-Care

Mental self-care is anything that keeps your mind working quickly and critically. It helps you cut through the fog of the day, week, or year and ensures that your quick wit and sharp mind are intact and working the way the cosmos intended. Making sure your mind is fit helps you problem-solve, decreases stress since you're not feeling overwhelmed, and keeps you feeling on top of your mental game—no matter your sign or your situation.

Spiritual Self-Care

Spiritual self-care is self-care that allows you to tap into your soul and the soul of the universe and uncover its secrets. Rather than focusing on a particular religion or set of religious beliefs, these types of self-care activities reconnect you with a higher power: the sense that something out there is bigger than you. When you meditate, you connect. When you pray, you connect. Whenever you do something that allows you to experience and marry yourself to the vastness that is the cosmos, you practice spiritual self-care.

Practical Self-Care

Self-care is what you do to take care of yourself, and practical self-care, while not as expansive as the other types, is made up of the seemingly small day-to-day tasks that bring you peace and accomplishment. These practical self-care rituals are important, but are often overlooked. Scheduling a doctor's appointment that you've been putting off is practical self-care. Getting your hair cut is practical self-care. Anything you can check off your list of things to be accomplished gives you a sacred space to breathe and allows the universe more room to bring a beautiful sense of cosmic fulfillment your way.

What Self-Care Isn't

Self-care is restorative. Self-care is clarifying. Self-care is whatever you need to do to make yourself feel secure in the universe.

Now that you know what self-care is, it's also important that you're able to see what self-care isn't. Self-care is not something that you force yourself to do because you think it will be good for you. Some signs are energy in motion and sitting still goes against their place in the universe. Those signs won't feel refreshed by lying in a hammock or sitting down to meditate. Other signs aren't able to ground themselves unless they've found a self-care practice that protects their cosmic need for peace and quiet. Those signs won't find parties, concerts, and loud venues soothing or satisfying. If a certain ritual doesn't bring you peace, clarity, or satisfaction, then it's not right for your sign and you should find something that speaks to you more clearly.

There's a difference though between not finding satisfaction in a ritual that you've tried and not wanting to try a self-care activity because you're tired or stuck in a comfort zone. Sometimes going to the gym or meeting up with friends is the self-care practice that you need to experience—whether engaging in it feels like a downer or not. So consider how you feel when you're actually doing the activity. If it feels invigorating to get on the treadmill or you feel delight when you actually catch up with your friend, the ritual is doing what it should be doing and clearing space for you—among other benefits...

The Benefits of Self-Care

The benefits of self-care are boundless and there's none that's superior to helping you put rituals in place to feel more at home in your body, in your spirit, and in your unique home in the cosmos. There are, however, other benefits to engaging in the practice of self-care that you should know.

Rejuvenates Your Immune System

No matter which rituals are designated for you by the stars, your sign, and its governing element, self-care helps both your body and mind rest, relax, and recuperate. The practice of self-care activates the parasympathetic nervous system (often called the rest and digest system), which slows your heart rate, calms the body, and, overall, helps your body relax and release tension. This act of decompression gives your body the space it needs to build up and strengthen your immune system, which protects you from illness.

Helps You Reconnect—with Yourself

When you practice the ritual of self-care—especially when you customize this practice based on your personal sign and governing element—you learn what you like to do and what you need to do to replenish yourself. Knowing yourself better, and allowing yourself the time and space that you need to focus on your personal needs and desires, gives you the gifts of self-confidence and self-knowledge. Setting time aside to focus on your needs also helps you put busy, must-do things aside, which gives you time to reconnect with yourself and who you are deep inside.

Increases Compassion

Perhaps one of the most important benefits of creating a self-care ritual is that, by focusing on yourself, you become more compassionate to others as well. When you truly take the time to care for yourself and make yourself and your importance in the universe a priority in your own life, you're then able to care for others and see their needs and desires in a new way. You can't pour from an empty dipper, and self-care allows you the space and clarity to do what you can to send compassion out into the world.

Starting a Self-Care Routine

Self-care should be treated as a ritual in your life, something you make the time to pause for, no matter what. You are important. You deserve rejuvenation and a sense of relaxation. You need to open your soul to the gifts that the universe is giving you, and self-care provides you with a way to ensure you're ready to receive those gifts. To begin a self-care routine, start by making yourself the priority. Do the customized rituals in Part 2 with intention, knowing the universe has already given them to you, by virtue of your sign and your governing element.

Now that you understand the role that self-care will hold in your life, let's take a closer look at the connection between self-care and astrology.

CHAPTER 2

SELF-CARE
AND ASTROLOGY

A strology is the study of the connection between the objects in the heavens (the planets,
the stars) and what happens here on earth. Just as
the movements of the planets and other heavenly
bodies influence the ebb and flow of the tides, so
do they influence you—your body, your mind, your
spirit. This relationship is ever present and is never
more important—or personal—than when viewed
through the lens of self-care.

In this chapter you'll learn how the locations of these celestial bodies at the time of your birth affect you and define the self-care activities that will speak directly to you as a Leo, an Aries, a Capricorn, or any of the other zodiac signs. You'll see how the zodiac influences every part of your being and why ignoring its lessons can leave you feeling frustrated and unfulfilled. You'll also realize that, when you perform the rituals of self-care based on your sign, the wisdom of the cosmos will lead you down a path of fulfillment and restoration—to the return of who you really are, deep inside.

Zodiac Polarities

In astrology, all signs are mirrored by other signs that are on the opposite side of the zodiac. This polarity ensures that the zodiac is balanced and continues to flow with an unbreakable, even stream of energy. There are two different polarities in the zodiac and each is called by a number of different names:

* Yang/masculine/positive polarity
* Yin/feminine/negative polarity

Each polar opposite embodies a number of opposing traits, qualities, and attributes that will influence which self-care practices will work for or against your sign and your own personal sense of cosmic balance.

Yang

Whether male or female, those who fall under yang, or masculine, signs are extroverted and radiate their energy outward. They are spontaneous, active, bold, and fearless. They move forward in life with the desire to enjoy everything the world has to offer to them, and they work hard to transfer their inspiration and positivity to others so that those individuals may experience the same gifts that the universe offers them. All signs governed by the fire and air elements are yang and hold the potential for these dominant qualities. We will refer to them with masculine pronouns. These signs are:

* Aries
* Leo
* Sagittarius

* Gemini
* Libra
* Aquarius

There are people who hold yang energy who are introverted and retiring. However, by practicing self-care that is customized for your sign and understanding the potential ways to use your energy, you can find a way—perhaps one that's unique to you—to claim your native buoyancy and dominance and engage with the path that the universe opens for you.

Yin

Whether male or female, those who fall under yin, or feminine, signs are introverted and radiate inwardly. They draw people and experiences to them rather than seeking people and experiences in an extroverted way. They move forward in life with an energy that is reflective, receptive, and focused on communication and achieving shared goals. All signs governed by the earth and water elements are yin and hold the potential for these reflective qualities. We will refer to them with feminine pronouns. These signs are:

* Taurus
* Virgo
* Capricorn

* Cancer
* Scorpio
* Pisces

As there are people with yang energy who are introverted and retiring, there are also people with yin energy who are outgoing and extroverted. And by practicing self-care rituals that speak to your particular sign, energy, and governing body, you will reveal your true self and the balance of energy will be maintained.

Governing Elements

Each astrological sign has a governing element that defines their energy orientation and influences both the way the sign moves through the universe and relates to self-care. The elements are fire, earth, air, and water. All the signs in each element share certain characteristics, along with having their own sign-specific qualities:

* **Fire:** Fire signs are adventurous, bold, and energetic. They enjoy the heat and warm environments and look to the sun and fire as a means to recharge their depleted batteries. They're competitive, outgoing, and passionate. The fire signs are Aries, Leo, and Sagittarius.
* **Earth:** Earth signs all share a common love and tendency toward a practical, material, sensual, and economic orientation. The earth signs are Taurus, Virgo, and Capricorn.
* **Air:** Air is the most ephemeral element and those born under this element are thinkers, innovators, and communicators. The air signs are Gemini, Libra, and Aquarius.
* **Water:** Water signs are instinctual, compassionate, sensitive, and emotional. The water signs are Cancer, Scorpio, and Pisces.

Chapter 3 teaches you all about the ways your specific governing element influences and drives your connection to your cosmically harmonious self-care rituals, but it's important that you realize how important these elemental traits are to your self-care practice and to the activities that will help restore and reveal your true self.

Sign Qualities

Each of the astrological elements governs three signs. Each of these three signs is also given its own quality or mode, which corresponds to a different part of each season: the beginning, the middle, or the end.

* **Cardinal signs:** The cardinal signs initiate and lead in each season. Like something that is just starting out, they are actionable, enterprising, and assertive, and are born leaders. The cardinal signs are Aries, Cancer, Libra, and Capricorn.
* **Fixed signs:** The fixed signs come into play when the season is well established. They are definite, consistent, reliable, motivated by principles, and powerfully stubborn. The fixed signs are Taurus, Leo, Scorpio, and Aquarius.
* **Mutable signs:** The mutable signs come to the forefront when the seasons are changing. They are part of one season, but also part of the next. They are adaptable, versatile, and flexible. The mutable signs are Gemini, Virgo, Sagittarius, and Pisces.

Each of these qualities tells you a lot about yourself and who you are. They also give you invaluable information about the types of self-care rituals that your sign will find the most intuitive and helpful.

Ruling Planets

In addition to qualities and elements, each specific sign is ruled by a particular planet that lends its personality to those born under that sign. Again, these sign-specific traits give you valuable insight into the personality of the signs and the self-care rituals that may best rejuvenate them. The signs that correspond to each planet—and the ways that those planetary influences determine your self-care options—are as follows:

* **Aries:** Ruled by Mars, Aries is passionate, energetic, and determined.
* **Taurus:** Ruled by Venus, Taurus is sensual, romantic, and fertile.
* **Gemini:** Ruled by Mercury, Gemini is intellectual, changeable, and talkative.
* **Cancer:** Ruled by the Moon, Cancer is nostalgic, emotional, and home loving.
* **Leo:** Ruled by the Sun, Leo is fiery, dramatic, and confident.
* **Virgo:** Ruled by Mercury, Virgo is intellectual, analytical, and responsive.
* **Libra:** Ruled by Venus, Libra is beautiful, romantic, and graceful.
* **Scorpio:** Ruled by Mars and Pluto, Scorpio is intense, powerful, and magnetic.

- **Sagittarius:** Ruled by Jupiter, Sagittarius is optimistic, boundless, and larger than life.
- **Capricorn:** Ruled by Saturn, Capricorn is wise, patient, and disciplined.
- **Aquarius:** Ruled by Uranus, Aquarius is independent, unique, and eccentric.
- **Pisces:** Ruled by Neptune and Jupiter, Pisces is dreamy, sympathetic, and idealistic.

A Word on Sun Signs

When someone is a Leo, Aries, Sagittarius, or any of the other zo diac signs, it means that the sun was positioned in this constellation in the heavens when they were born. Your Sun sign is a dominant factor in defining your personality, your best self-care practices, and your soul nature. Every person also has the position of the Moon, Mercury, Venus, Mars, Jupiter, Saturn, Uranus, Neptune, and Pluto. These planets can be in any of the elements: fire signs, earth signs, air signs, or water signs. If you have your entire chart calculated by an astrologer or on an Internet site, you can see the whole picture and learn about all your elements. Someone born under Leo with many signs in another element will not be as concentrated in the fire element as someone with five or six planets in Leo. Someone born in Pisces with many signs in another element will not be as concentrated in the water element as someone with five or six planets in Pisces. And so on. Astrology is a complex system and has many shades of meaning. For our purposes, looking at the self-care practices designated by your Sun sign, or what most people con- sider *their* sign, will give you the information you need to move forward and find fulfillment and restoration.

CHAPTER 3

ESSENTIAL ELEMENTS: AIR

The air element is perhaps the most elusive element of the zodiac. Air is everywhere, invisible, and yet completely necessary for life. We are so sensitive to air that we even feel a momentary change in the currents around us or the amount of oxygen in our body.

In astrology, air is the third element of creation, preceded by earth and fire. The air signs (Gemini, Libra, and Aquarius) are the thinkers of the zodiac. Their dominion is mental—the realm of ideas and concepts. For example, you may have heard the saying that a person "builds castles in the air" or "has his head in the clouds." These statements are usually made as pejorative expressions, but for air signs they describe the essence of who they are. Air signs live in a world of both rational and intuitive thought. They are imaginative and dream, sometimes idealistically, of new and better ways to be, to think, and to communicate. Any self-care they do must reflect that disposition as well. Let's take a look at the mythological importance of air and its counterparts, the basic characteristics of the three air signs, and what they all have in common when it comes to self-care.

The Mythology of Air

In Greek mythology the legend of Icarus has a symbolic meaning with the air element. In this myth Icarus and his father, Daedalus, a talented Athenian craftsman responsible for building a labyrinth for King Minos to imprison the Minotaur, were themselves imprisoned in the labyrinth in Crete for crimes against the king. To escape the Minotaur, Daedalus fashioned wings of wax and feathers that he and his son could use to fly over the sea. Daedalus warned his son not to fly too near the sun as the heat would cause his wings to melt. But Icarus became enchanted by his freedom and flew too close to the sun. Soon, the wax melted and Icarus fell into the sea.

The lesson for the air signs in this myth is that going beyond sense and reason usually does not work out. In the case of

Icarus, he followed his desire instead of his rational side, and ended up falling to his death. Ideas are wonderful—they are the foundation of many great creations. But for air signs, ideas are followed by the hard work of grounding them in physical reality. Self-care rituals that cater to both mind and heart are key for air signs, but balance and rationale are often paramount.

The Element of Air

Air signs are known for their curiosity, pursuit of knowledge, and keen ability to communicate. They delight in conversation and feel most passionate when they are confronting a dilemma of the mind straight on. But their grand ideas sometimes make them unpredictable. Because of this, they must be challenged in all parts of their lives. Doing the same thing over and over will just leave them bored. This goes for self-care as well. They need variety and different options for wellness activities, or they may not participate at all. Air signs are buoyant, perceptive, and inventive. For example, Gemini is expressive and always ready to entertain. Libra is gentle and will listen to a friend's troubles for hours. And Aquarius is ingenious, helping to solve problems with different approaches.

Astrological Symbols

The astrological symbols (also called the zodiacal symbols) of the air signs also give you hints as to how air signs move through the world. Each symbol ties back to the analytical, curious nature associated with air signs:

* Gemini is the Twins
* Libra is the Scales
* Aquarius is the Water Bearer

All these signs show intimate harmony with the cycles of the seasons and a personal connection with air. Gemini represents duality of the mind, and his symbol resembles the Roman numeral two. Libra brings balance with his scales of justice. And Aquarius represents positive movement and nourishment with waves of water or electricity. Each air sign's personality and subsequent approaches to self-care tie back to the qualities of these symbols.

Signs and Seasonal Modes

Each of the elements in astrology has a sign that corresponds to a different part of each season.

* **Fixed:** Aquarius is a fixed air sign. He rules in winter. The fixed signs are definite, motivated by principles, and powerfully stubborn.
* **Mutable:** Gemini is the first air sign and marks the end of spring and the beginning of summer. Gemini is called a mutable air sign because he ushers us from one season to the next. Mutable signs are changeable and flexible.
* **Cardinal:** Libra, the second air sign, occurs in autumn; he is the cardinal air sign because the autumn equinox occurs around Libra's time. The cardinal signs are leaders and action-oriented.

If you know your element and whether you are a cardinal, fixed, or mutable sign, you know a lot about yourself. This is invaluable for self-care and is reflected in the customized air sign self-care rituals found in Part 2.

Air Signs and Self-Care

When it comes to self-care, air signs must realize that they have a very sensitive nervous system. Not only do they react to changes in the weather and the "vibrations" around them in social situations, they also react to the power of words and ideas. Sometimes, they are not aware that their words can wound others, but they are always aware when someone says something hurtful to them. However, air signs are not a feeling sign, they are a thinking sign. They perceive that they are angry or hurt, but their feelings are expressed more in terms of the other person's actions, so they'll respond with "I thought that was rude," or "how unkind and cruel." Self-care must involve tapping into their emotions as well as the logic that precedes them.

Air signs are not oriented toward the physical. For instance, they know they have to eat and take care of their health, but the action comes second to thinking about it all. They can lose track of time and forget that they only had a croissant for breakfast! The first part of any self-care program for air signs is to understand the concept that self-care is a good thing to do for an easier and more productive life. Long-range thinking is an air sign specialty, so why not apply it to long-range self-care goals? This makes intuitive sense to air signs. In this way the most successful self-care activities should be interesting and involve an overall concept, such as "If I do this, I will learn some new ways of understanding myself and others," or "This is a new therapy that promises to eliminate my posture problem. I will check it out." Just doing something is not enough—air signs want to be sure of their reasons.

Repeating meaningless habits is a pitfall for air signs. If they get stuck in a rut, they'll ditch their self-care and run off to a party instead. Air signs are creative, and the same effort they exert for a nice dinner, social outing, story, or song should also apply to self-care. On the flip side, any activity or program that is cumbersome won't last long with air signs. If there is too much equipment to deal with or too much effort to get to that particular gym or hiking trail, the air sign just won't do it.

Air signs have an aesthetic sense in all aspects of their lives, which is why any self-care activity has to be effective as well as pleasing to the eye. For example, a diet plan must be tasty and involve food that is beautifully displayed. Those two qualities please air signs and will motivate them. The plan also has to be simple to follow. No elaborate timetables, just clear directions.

So now that you know what air signs need to practice self-care, let's look at each of the unique characteristics of Aquarius and how he can maintain his gifts.

CHAPTER 4

SELF-CARE FOR AQUARIUS

Dates: January 20–February 18
Element: Air
Polarity: Yang
Quality: Fixed
Symbol: Water Bearer
Ruler: Uranus

Aquarius is the most unpredictable sign of the zodiac. He is the sign of invention, individuality, group consciousness, and genius. There are two distinct Aquarian personality types because before the discovery of Uranus, Aquarius was ruled by cautious and conservative Saturn. Ancient astrologers had predicted a planet farther out than Saturn that could not be seen by the naked eye.

They called this planet Ouranos, after the mythological sky god. With the electrifying discovery of Uranus by William Herschel in 1781, astronomers verified what ancient astrologers had predicted.

Astrologers then observed that many people born under the sign of Aquarius had characteristics that were not Saturnine, but something different. These characteristics are now called Uranian, and they speak to the uniqueness and future-oriented personality of this most individual sign. Today, as we move toward the Age of Aquarius, we see some Aquarians who harken back to Saturnine influences, but the majority (especially among the last two generations) are those who are moving forward into the unknown, unpredictable excitement of Uranus's influence.

The planet Uranus in mythology was symbolized by Ouranos, the sky god, who had an unusual and dramatic debut in the pantheon of the gods. His mother was the Earth Mother, Gaia, who emerged from chaos and gave birth to Ouranos (who was both her husband and son). Their relationship was so passionate that Gaia could not give birth to their children. One of Gaia's children was Cronos, who in Roman astrology was called Saturn. Cronos decided to overthrow Ouranos and, while in the womb, emasculated his father. Ouranos later regained prominence, but his shattering beginnings are symbolic of the Aquarian rebellious and antiauthoritarian streak.

Aquarius is an air sign, and his symbol confuses some people. His sign is called the Water Bearer, and the symbol shows a young boy pouring something that looks like water from a large vase. Ancient sources record that when the constellation of Aquarius rose in Egypt and Babylonia, it corresponded with a period of floods and rain; hence, the symbol may pertain to weather patterns in the ancient world.

The symbol, however, also symbolically portrays the youth pouring rays of knowledge for all humanity. Aquarius's purpose, astrologically speaking, is to pour forth knowledge and ideas that benefit all people. For example, the Internet is Aquarius ruled and a perfect example of individual ingenuity in service of the collective. The Internet is also theoretically equalitarian, a cherished value for Aquarius.

The planet Uranus represents the breakthrough force that shatters old forms. Aquarius's soul mission is to coordinate spirit and matter in new and revolutionary ways. His humanitarian principles can lead him to promote actions that are personally beneficial and beneficial for humanity. He thinks and acts for others as though they were all joined together in the common endeavor of living on this planet...which, in fact, we are.

Self-Care and Aquarius

Of all the air signs Aquarius is the most blasé about self-care. He has a sensitive nervous system, but doesn't like to get bogged down in physical minutia. He lives in future possibilities and frequently can forget that the here and now requires tending. Aquarius also has an "electric" nervous system that is erratic: he is either on or off. It is as if someone pulled the plug on his energies when they are off, but when he is on, it's like someone ramped up his voltage. Tuning into this rhythm is essential for Aquarius self-care.

One of the manifestations of Aquarius's supercharged mental activity is insomnia. It can come in waves or be chronic. Physical exercise is very good for balancing the energy, as is meditation and breathing exercises. But if Aquarius is riding the wave of creativity, it is best for him to go with it and sleep when the inspiration wanes. Some Aquarians simply do not need as much sleep as other people do.

Taking drugs to sleep or relax is often a bad idea, but especially so for Aquarius. Dampening his natural spirit shuts down his imagination. Over time he can become lethargic and dull because his life flow energy has been thwarted.

Aquarius, like all air signs, is a thinking sign rather than a feeling sign. He often has a detached quality and does not understand his more emotional brothers and sisters. It is as if feeling people are speaking another language. Like Spock in Star Trek, to him emotions are illogical and get in the way of useful activities that could improve any situation. However, the more evolved Aquarius understands and respects the intuitive knowledge that the more feeling signs have. The Aquarian may not be a gushy person, but he can learn to respect those qualities in others. Those Aquarians who remain detached can sometimes come off as cruel, distant, and impossible to sway.

Aquarius is the sign of the rebel. He doesn't like constraints. Self-care wise, this is a problematic impulse. But, if Aquarius thinks, "I could have much more impact on the world if I were fitter or ate better," that is the opening into motivation for his self-care. Aquarius is not lusting for fame or fortune necessarily, but he needs to know that his ideas are traveling to other people (like the rays of knowledge in his symbol).

Aquarius might start a blog about whether or not self-care is productive for the planet. For example, the statistics on meat eating and the amount of energy it consumes might sway Aquarius to become a vegetarian. Doing something good for humanity is more of a motivator than self-care for his own sake. This is not altruism—just an indication that he is interested in breaking through standard practices that are outmoded and potentially harmful to the group as a whole.

Aquarius Rules the Circulation

Aquarius rules the circulation of blood and energy, as well as the calves and ankles. In Chinese medicine the life force of the body is called chi. Acupuncture and acupressure techniques balance chi to restore health to the whole body. It is a very old practice and particularly beneficial to Aquarius, as his energy can get dammed up and cause circulatory problems.

The ankles are also vulnerable to stress for Aquarius. An Aquarius jogger should tape his ankles to increase his strength. Activities such as in-line skating, ice-skating, or snowboarding require special care to keep Aquarius's ankles strong and injury-free. A muscle-building exercise that can help is to work with leg weights in the exercise room.

Sports and exercise are essential for Aquarius to keep blood and energy moving. He excels at both team and individual sports. In fact, among the top fifty athletes of all time, Aquarius is the most represented sign. Aquarian athletes apportion their energy well and enjoy the flow.

Mindless aerobics or exercise classes are not good outlets for bursts of Uranian energy. Aquarius gets bored, and repetitive motion actually tenses his muscles. If he is in an exercise rut because he thinks it is good for him, then he can cause himself physical damage with these repetitions. The best exercise choices for him are martial arts, Bikram yoga, jazz dancing, and Zumba.

Psychologically, Aquarius may have a hard time with therapy because he resents anyone trying to "normalize" him. If a therapist says, "Well, this is the way the world works," Aquarius just doesn't believe it and walks. Aquarius is not abnormal, but definitely marches to the beat of a different drummer. Counseling that incorporates methods such as cognitive behavioral therapy, neuro-linguistic programming (NLP), or hypnotherapy could be more beneficial than classic therapy. Aquarius has to be sold on the need to do therapy and the type of therapy he will engage in. He generally wants to solve a problem, not get lost in stories of his childhood or difficulties. Besides, Aquarius can think himself imaginatively in and out of problems, so he may think he can cut out the middle man and skip the therapy.

Aquarius and Self-Care Success

Consistency in anything is usually not Aquarius's forte. If he is in an active phase, then a new self-care program would be appealing. However, if he is off, nothing will motivate him to do the things he knows he should. He truly resents thinking that he should do anything. He is not lazy, just too busy doing something else. Once he can place taking care of himself in a broader context, then he can be disciplined: self-care becomes self-knowledge and might even benefit other people!

Self-care is productive when Aquarius can follow his own rhythm. Consistency usually doesn't work, but over time with activity and fallow times, he gets the job done.

In self-care, he is also not swayed by socializing routinely with groups, although he advocates group activities. For Aquarius boring people are cautious and regular about self-care. If Aquarius finds a group that enlightens and challenges him, then he will be part of it and probably will become the leader. Leading his own self-care New Age group is the single best way for Aquarius to take care of himself. It partners with the idea of everyone working together, plus he benefits personally.

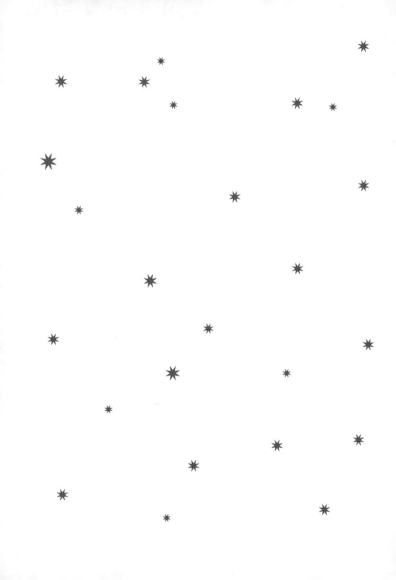

PART 2

SELF-CARE
RITUALS
— FOR —
AQUARIUS

Join an Exotic Food Club

One of Aquarius's fun qualities is a love of experimentation and trying new things. Apply that trait to your diet and find a way to explore new flavors and tastes regularly.

You can join a convenient subscription-based club that sends new foods right to your door once a month, or go to a local meeting of a group of people who like to try unique foods. (They might meet after work once a month for a quick meal, offer weekend dates for longer tasting sessions, or rent out restaurants for special events.) Search online for such groups and ask the moderator if you can join. Your adventurous personality will likely be a perfect fit!

Go Cloud-Watching

A ir signs are intellectual thinkers who excel at
creative thought and problem-solving. But sometimes that can mean it's hard to turn off your racing
mind. If you're having trouble figuring out the answer
to a question, take care of yourself today by taking a
well-deserved break to clear your mind. Need something else to focus on? Look up at the clouds. Take
some time to lie back and watch the clouds move
through the sky. You're sure to feel refreshed and
will be able to look at any challenges with a fresh
perspective.

Clear Your Mind
with Meditation

We've all heard about the many benefits of meditation: it can reduce stress, depression, and anxiety; increase happiness, focus, and self-awareness; and even improve your physical health. Some research has indicated that meditation can be helpful for everything from minor aches and pains and even the simple headache to major illnesses—including asthma, chronic pain, heart conditions, and cancer. Meditation is a perfect activity for air signs, who can use it to find balance and harmony in their everyday lives.

Use your meditation practice as an opportunity to stop overthinking and redirect your attention. Meditation will allow you to clear your mind and breathe, so you'll stay emotionally and physically healthy.

Use Writing Prompts

A ir signs are often creative and great at expression. Why not try channeling those skills into some writing? Some well-known authors such as Shel Silverstein, Oscar Wilde, Charles Dickens, and Judy Blume were able to channel their air sign qualities into incredible literary works—maybe you can too!

Not sure where to start? Writing prompts are a great way to boost your creativity and give you the kind of challenge you love. Look for a writing prompt book at your local library, or check out different social media communities for ideas to help you get started.

Cleanse Your Home by Smudging

The state of your mind is often reflected in the state of your home. If there's clutter everywhere and dust is starting to gather, there's a good chance you're feeling stuck emotionally and mentally as well. For intellectual air signs, this clutter can make you feel unbalanced and distressed. Smudging is a simple cleansing ritual that you can use to clear out negativity in your home (and also your mind!) and inspire a fresh, positive start.

All you'll need to get started is some ceremonial sage (not the type found in the spice aisle at grocery stores) or palo santo sticks, a fireproof bowl, and some matches or a lighter. Tidy up any obvious clutter and open as many doors and windows as possible in your home. Place the sage or palo santo in a fireproof bowl and light the stick. Blow it out and use the fireproof bowl to hold the smoking stick as you walk around your home, spreading the smoke throughout and focusing on its ability to remove negativity. Make way for a refreshed, positive attitude!

Try the Camel Pose

The Camel Pose is a backbend posture that can improve circulation, which is especially important for Aquarius. Camel Pose also stretches the whole front of your body and can feel energizing after you've been sitting for a long period of time. This is not a beginner's pose, so make sure to practice this with your yoga instructor for technique guidance.

To do the pose, kneel down on a yoga mat with the tops of your feet pressed into the mat. Rest your hands on your lower back and gently lean back toward your feet. If you are flexible enough, you can then reach back and touch or hold each heel with your hands. And, if it feels comfortable, allow your head to drop back without straining your neck. Hold the pose for about three breaths (or whatever feels comfortable), then slowly come up, bringing your head forward last. Breathe deeply.

Feed the Birds

All birds are friends to air signs—they share your free-spirited nature! You may find it soothing and calming to watch birds fly about. Why not encourage them to come to your yard by setting up a bird feeder? Different birds will like different foods, so try putting out a seed mix, suet, or even the popular black oil sunflower seed that attracts many different kinds of birds. Make sure to place your feeder in a safe place away from predators and windows. You may even want to get expert advice on adopting (and properly caring for) a parakeet, mynah bird, or canary as a pet from a local animal shelter!

Enjoy Some Green Tea

Air signs are curious and great at solving problems—but that can also mean that they're chronic overthinkers as well. Give yourself a restorative break to clear your mind and reframe your mind-set. Not sure how to begin? Try making it a habit to drink a peaceful cup of green tea every day; mix it up with some fruit-flavored or jasmine green teas for a little variety. Use your daily cup of tea as a chance to clear your mind and take a break from worrying about anything stressful in your life. (If you have health problems or are on medication, check with your doctor first.)

Afterward, you're sure to find you feel more relaxed and rejuvenated and ready to take on any challenges that come your way. Bring your tea outside for the added benefit of a little fresh air on your break!

Learn about the Weather

––––––––––––––

Air signs are sensitive to changes in the weather, so you're already likely to be very aware of the changes in the air around you. You can encourage your intellectual interests and take better care of your physical self by learning a little more about the weather. Purchase an old-fashioned barometer to keep in your home.

A barometer is a scientific instrument that's often used to predict the weather because it measures changes in the atmospheric pressure. High pressure usually indicates good weather, but watch out if that level starts to drop! Not only will you learn a fun new piece of information to share, you'll also be prepared no matter the weather with just a glance at your barometer.

Recite a Mantra

Mantras are positive words or phrases that you can repeat aloud or to yourself to improve your self-confidence and motivation. Best of all they're easy to work into your day—you can say them in the shower, in your head during your commute, or when you're meditating.

Because Aquarius is so unique, sometimes the world might try to convince you to stop being you and instead join the crowd. When you need reassurance that your special qualities shouldn't be silenced, repeat "I go my own way" as you breathe deeply. Your individuality is something you should celebrate and cultivate, and these powerful words can remind you of that if you're feeling doubtful.

Grow Purifying Houseplants

Did you know that plants can help purify the air around you? Try bringing some houseplants into your home to help improve the air quality. English ivy, bamboo palm, and peace lilies are all beautiful houseplants that will help remove airborne toxins from your home. There are plenty of other options, however, so do some research to see what will grow well in your home. Warning, though, some plants are poisonous to house pets, so make sure to take the needs of your furry friends into consideration as well. Choose the plants that work best for you, and, as an air sign, you will feel your best and most balanced around these natural air purifiers.

Take Yourself to the Movies

Air signs love learning about new ideas, and a great way to do so is to head to the movies. Treat yourself to a couple of hours of comfortable seating, buttery popcorn, and an interesting new movie. You might try checking out a documentary or something that's particularly thought-provoking.

Although it's always fun to bring friends to the movie theater, you might consider making the occasional trip alone. Air signs appreciate the opportunity to think deeply about things they've learned. Enjoy the time alone to really analyze and fully process the movie you've just seen.

Carry an Aquamarine
Stone with You

————————————

Crystals and gemstones have a powerful connection with the energy of the earth, which itself is made up of rocks and matter from all over the universe.

Even though he is an air sign, Aquarius is also closely tied to water, and water's light blue-green color is reflected in the aquamarine stone. Aquamarine is known to refresh your outlook and strengthen your sense of community. You can carry a raw piece of this stone around with you, wear it as jewelry, or place a polished piece in your home as décor.

Host a Game Night

Air signs love to be social, and that social inter-action is all they need to spark some happiness and excitement into their everyday lives! You're likely well known for being great company, so grab some snacks, pull out your favorite games, and invite some friends over for game night! Some friendly compe-tition and interesting conversations will help you reconnect with friends you haven't seen in a while.

For some added air sign fun, look for word-based games that will play to your language-loving strengths. Scrabble, Boggle, and Bananagrams are all popular options, but there are plenty of lesser known variations that you might enjoy.

Dye Your Hair a Crazy Color

Getting bored with your regular hair color? Embrace your daring streak and dye your hair with streaks of a bold color like purple or blue. You can visit a hair color professional to do the job or grab an at-home kit at a drugstore if you're feeling brave (make sure to follow all the instructions carefully).

Changing your hair color will keep your life fresh and help you feel like you're embracing who you really are—a rebel! You might even inspire others to try something similar when they see how great your hair looks.

Hang Out in a Hammock

As an air sign, it's important for you to get outside and get some fresh air. One great way to unwind and recharge outside is to relax in a hammock. Enjoy rocking in the breeze and give yourself permission to take a quick mental break. You can chat with friends nearby or spend some time by yourself, appreciating the nature around you. You should even feel free to close your eyes and take a little nap—you'll feel incredibly relaxed when you wake up! But if you're still in need of some mental stimulation to distract yourself, bring a book with you and take a little time to read. Your intellectual side will thank you!

Visit a Psychic

There's something so intriguing about visiting a psychic to see what the future holds for you. Aquarius in particular is always curious about what might happen down the road, so this activity might pique your interest since you're open to all sorts of ways to learn about the world.

Ask friends or look online for a recommended psychic who can open your eyes to what might be in store in the years ahead. You might learn something you never knew about yourself or revive an old goal or dream you've let fall by the wayside. Either way you're in for an exciting visit!

Make Art at Midnight

Yes, you need your sleep, and it's important to rest when you feel tired. But Aquarius's superactive mind can also be plagued by insomnia every once in a while. When those bouts hit, experts advise that you get out of bed and do a soothing activity to calm your racing thoughts.

For Aquarius this is a great time to tap into your creativity and paint, draw, write, or try some other quiet pursuit. Keeping your hands busy will lessen the stress of not sleeping, and allowing your mind to wander as you freewrite or paint might make you feel drowsy eventually. You'll climb back into bed exhausted and wake up to the masterpiece you created!

Be Weird

In a sea of boring gray fish swimming in the same direction, you're a riot of color swimming the other way. While this uniqueness is something to revel in, it can also draw unwanted feedback from those gray fish. In these moments remind yourself that you are a gift, and you're perfect just as you are. What other people see as weird or different is actually exactly what makes you so special.

The truth is that Aquarius can be eccentric, but it's better to embrace and flaunt that trait than to try to hide it. The world needs a little color, and you're just the person to provide it.

Clear Space in Your Home

Air signs may seem like they're in constant motion. And that's certainly true of their minds, which are often off and running to solve whatever problems come their way. Yet sometimes air signs can get thrown off—both physically and mentally—by stagnant air in their home.

If you start feeling stuck or out of balance, get rid of anything old or musty in your home or apartment. Also consider rearranging the furniture, as moving furniture allows the air to circulate more easily through your living spaces. Your thoughts will mimic the newly refreshed space and be able to flow more freely.

Analyze Your Handwriting

———————

With the air signs' interest in communication, they're likely to appreciate the importance of writing and may be very interested in what they can learn from their own handwriting. Your handwriting could be an important key to revealing some interesting aspects of your personality. Things like the slant, size, and thickness of your letters can be important, so have your handwriting analyzed! For instance, did you know that large letters indicate a big personality? If your handwriting slants to the right, you might like to meet new people. Learn some basic handwriting analysis tricks and practice your new skills with your friends to see if you can get to know them better!

Go on a Weekly Hike

Air signs need to spend plenty of time out in the fresh air, so they're likely to feel reenergized after heading out for a hike. If you go out to the woods or fields, you'll get a chance to view some beautiful scenery while you walk.

You can also combine your appreciation for the outdoors with your workout schedule! Hiking is a great workout that can improve heart health, strengthen muscles, and increase stability and balance. It's also often recommended as a natural stress-relief activity. It's just as important to take care of your body as it is your mind, so add a weekly hike to your workouts!

Travel the World

Air signs may seem as if they're always on the move, so think about places you might like to visit to actually get yourself moving. It's always a good idea to have a trip planned for the near future. You don't have to go far or plan an extensive, expensive vacation, but a nice weekend away or a few nights in a place you've always wanted to visit can give you something to look forward to and keep your energy high. Try visiting someplace peaceful to give yourself a chance to recharge, or research places you could visit to add an intellectual element to your next trip, like cities with interesting museums or historical monuments. Your adventurous free spirit will appreciate the change of scenery.

Try Acupuncture

Acupuncture is a method of traditional Chinese medicine, which involves a trained practitioner inserting tiny needles into specific points on the body to treat a wide variety of health issues. It's based on the concept that the energy, or chi, in your body needs to flow freely and be balanced in order for you to feel well. When your energy is blocked or imbalanced, you feel physically ill or mentally out of sorts.

Acupuncture is especially useful for Aquarius because his energy has a tendency to get dammed up, causing circulation problems. Find a local skilled acupuncturist, and try it out the next time you don't feel well. Explain your issue to the practitioner, and they will arrange a personalized session that focuses on your specific concerns.

Protect Your Ankles

Aquarius rules the ankles, so you need to make sure you take good care of yours. If you play sports that put strain on your ankles—such as skating, skiing, snowboarding, and running—visit a sports medicine facility to ask experts the best way to take care of your ankles both in the short and long term. Ask if you should wear stretchy braces or tape your ankles to give them extra support. You can also learn specialized stretches, precise healing methods, and preventative exercises to keep your ankles in top shape for years to come.

Listen to Conversation Around You

Air signs are the element of communication, so it's only natural for you to pay attention to the conversations around you. You're also always ready to learn new things, so you're likely to be listening for subjects that might pique your interest. Whether you're riding the subway, waiting in line at the supermarket, or mingling at a party, you're sure to catch some snippets of chatter that grab your attention. You might even consider carrying around a notebook and pen to jot down little bits of conversation you hear or interesting topics you'd like to learn more about later.

Consider Alternatives to Traditional Therapy

Traditional talk therapy is a great resource for some people. But Aquarius might have a harder time aligning with that particular method because of his reluctance to have anyone tell him what's "normal" or "typical."

That doesn't mean that you should bottle up your feelings either though. Instead, trying therapy that incorporates cognitive behavioral therapy, hypno-therapy, or neuro-linguistic programming (NLP) might be more of a match for your personality. They are all innovative ways to change behavior. These methods are particularly effective at purposeful problem-solving (not necessarily diving into long-ago childhood stories), which is usually in line with Aquarius's preferences. Make sure to ask your primary care physician for a local recommendation, and try one of these therapies for a mental health check-in.

Visit Some Butterflies

Air signs can be spontaneous and would love to head out on an airy getaway. Try visiting a butterfly sanctuary! A butterfly sanctuary is an indoor living space or conservatory designed specifically for the breeding, development, and safe display of butterflies. They also offer lots of opportunities to learn about the butterflies and the ways we can conserve and protect them!

This visit can be a great opportunity to take care of yourself physically since you can spend plenty of time walking around the garden areas. This enjoyable activity can also have emotional benefits. Your positive mood is sure to carry through into your day well after you leave the sanctuary.

Color Outside the Lines

The adult coloring book craze seems to celebrate very traditional coloring—applying perfect shades of grass green, staying within the outer lines of the picture, using amazing types of shading and intricacy. And that's certainly one way to color.

But the Aquarius way is to forget all those "rules" and color your way. Make the grass bright blue. Turn the page upside down. Rip a page out, cut it in half, and connect it to another half-page to make a unique picture. Push color beyond the boundaries of the design in any way that speaks to you. This way of coloring is still meditative and calming—it just better reflects your Aquarius personality.

Continue Your Education

Air signs are the intellectuals of the zodiac and are always looking to learn something new. Continue your education by pursuing an advanced degree. By doing so, you'll be practicing good mental self-care through fully engaging in an intellectual pursuit. However, you might also find some practical benefits to continuing your education. By pursuing a degree in your field, you may discover that you're better qualified for a different position in your company. Or, if you choose to expand your horizons and go for a new degree in an entirely different field, you might be able to move into a new dream job.

Update Your Home Décor

If it's been a while since you've refreshed your living space, now is a perfect time to do it. You'll make your home more reflective of who you are, more energizing, and more restorative.

Aquarius need not hold back on bold or unique décor—anything's fair game! Aquarius likes all neon colors, so look for iridescent accents to brighten darker corners of your space. A disco ball in your entry can cast a cool light pattern that will catch your eye and make you smile. The motion of a twirling gyroscope on your coffee table can also help you relax. When you've finished decorating, hold a house re-warming party to share your new space with friends and family.

Stop Gossiping

Because air signs are so great at communication, people really enjoy talking to them. That can be great news—you love speaking to and learning from a lot of people—but you need to be careful with everything you learn. People will often feel comfortable sharing their personal issues with you, and it's up to you to be respectful of that. Avoid gossiping, and don't share anyone's personal information without their permission. For someone as social as you are, it's important that you keep your friendships in good shape. Your friends trust you, so remember to honor their feelings to keep your relationships going strong.

Find Balance Through Reiki

———————————

Sometimes an air sign can become unbalanced, perhaps due to overthinking or an issue with communication. When unbalanced, you may have difficulty being open-minded and feel unwilling to accept new ideas—or you may feel overwhelmed with options. A Reiki treatment can be useful for reestablishing order in your life.

Reiki is a healing technique that aims to improve the movement of energy throughout the body through gentle touch. A Reiki session can cleanse your energy so it flows through your body smoothly and gets you back into balance. This practice will help you feel revitalized and refreshed, so be sure to consider setting up a session during high-stress times.

Head Out on an Adventure

A ir signs have an adventurous side, and you're known among your friends for being fun and spontaneous. If you're feeling a little bored lately, seek out some new experiences to recharge yourself and give you the excitement you need. Go for something a little unexpected with some wild (but still air-themed!) fun. Take a ride in a hot-air balloon to view your home from an entirely new perspective. Take a class to learn how to swing high on a trapeze for a unique workout. Or head out for a weekend away from home to learn kitesurfing from an expert. Give yourself the boost you need to keep your energy up!

Embrace Your Inner Unicorn

Unicorns may be mythical, but they still symbolize the purity of Aquarian ideals. Therefore, try to incorporate unicorns in your life in one way or another. It shouldn't be too difficult—unicorns are currently a favorite theme in décor and clothing.

You can put unicorn stickers or decals in your bedroom or bathroom, or grab a tote bag or T-shirt with a unicorn on it. If you're feeling more cultured, take a special trip to visit The Met Cloisters (a museum in New York City that specializes in medieval arts), where you can see a beautiful decorative medieval tapestry that features unicorns.

Celebrate Your Alone Time

A ir signs are very social and are known for being great company because they can keep any situation from becoming too boring. However, it's important that you don't let yourself get burned out by spending all your time keeping other people entertained. It's good to take some time for yourself! Appreciate the time you have to spend doing something you like, whether that's heading outdoors or learning something new. Taking time to concentrate on yourself will give you a positive outlook and a fresh perspective. So instead of always focusing on others, reframe your mind-set and simply enjoy being alone.

Keep Your Windows Open

Your home should be a place for you to relax, recharge, and reconnect with yourself. So make sure to pay homage to your air sign qualities in your home décor. Whether you live in a house or apartment, you'll be happiest and most comfortable with lots of windows that open. Try to keep your windows open all year long, especially after a cold spell or heat wave. Even if you have central air or heat, it can be helpful to keep just one window open. Changing the air currents changes the energy in your home, so be sure to let fresh air and positive energy flow throughout your living space.

Relax with a Guided
Sleep Meditation

Aquarius can sometimes grapple with insomnia.
If you run into this issue, one solution is a
guided meditation specifically designed to help you
feel drowsy.

You can find many options by searching online or
on *YouTube*, or check your local library if you need
a CD version. You could start with a general sleep
theme, or look for one that addresses specific needs,
like releasing worries or repeating positive affirma-
tions. When you need to sleep, turn on the meditation,
lie down, and breathe deeply while you listen and drift
off to a restful slumber.

Wear Batik Fabric

Batik is typically a type of Indonesian fabric made by applying wax to certain sections of the fabric, then dyeing the rest. The areas that had wax do not accept the color and thus you can make lots of intricate patterns. It is an ingenious way of creating a very individual fabric. Batik suits Aquarius because of its bold color palette and unique designs.

In addition to wearing batik clothing, you could also plan a fabulous trip to tropical Bali, one place where this gorgeous fabric is made. Visit local studios there to see the rich fabrics being created right in front of your eyes—or ask for some expert instruction and assist in making your own personalized design and color scheme!

Enjoy the Morning Crossword

Sometimes, doing something to keep your mind sharp is an important way to take care of yourself. Successfully completing a challenging task can help you feel stimulated and ready to take on the next project that comes your way. For air signs who love language and are often great problem-solvers, a crossword puzzle is a great way to exercise your mind. A word puzzle also has the added benefit of helping you learn new vocabulary, which air signs will love. Establish a new daily ritual and try doing your crossword puzzle in the morning—your success will help set the positive tone for the rest of the day!

Flaunt Iridescent Colors

That shimmery, multicolored shade you see on certain seashells and soap bubbles is iridescence—and it's a great match for Aquarius. The unique way iridescent materials look when light hits them represents your individuality and eccentricity.

Whether you wear iridescent accessories like cuff links or gemstone bracelets, or go bold and don a shimmery iridescent minidress or shirt, you're sure to garner compliments and turn heads. Iridescent home décor is also a good option—look for modern picture frames, sparkly hanging charms, or a shimmery shower curtain. Iridescence is timeless, spellbinding, and unique—just like you.

Subscribe to New Podcasts

———————————————

There are all kinds of ways to learn new information, and air signs are especially good at learning by listening. A great way for you to gather more information might be through podcasts. Podcasts are perfect for when you're on the go, since you can listen wherever you are, whether you're driving, grocery shopping, or even working out. There's a lot to learn, so choose a topic that you find interesting and simply search for the right podcast for you!

Listening to a podcast can also be a nice mental break. Centering your thoughts on whatever you're listening to can help you relax and redirect your mind away from any problem that's worrying you.

Dine Alfresco

_____

Remember, fresh air is vital for air signs, so it's important to reclaim that outdoor time for yourself. Free-spirited air signs appreciate a little spontaneous fun; try to be creative about how you find that time. For example, why not eat outdoors? Whether you're spending the day at the beach or boardwalk or going on a picnic in the park, enjoying a healthy meal outdoors can be great for your physical and mental well-being. If you don't have time for an all-day event, you can still head outdoors by asking to be seated outside at a restaurant or even bringing a home-cooked meal out onto your own patio or deck.

Practice Aromatherapy

Relaxing with special scents is a great way to disconnect from a busy day and calm your mind. You can diffuse essential oils through reeds or other diffusers. Patchouli and spike lavender in particular are effective scents for Aquarius.

Patchouli's musky, earthy scent is able to help drive out negative energy. Spike lavender (also called Portuguese lavender) has a fresh, floral scent with hints of camphor. It's known to help relieve headaches and induce relaxation, which is good if you're having trouble sleeping.

Keep In Touch with Friends

Air signs are great at intercommunication, and it's important for their well-being to have that social interaction throughout their lives. Other signs though? Not so much. Before you get upset that you haven't heard from your friends in a while, try making the first move and reaching out. Send a quick text to a friend you haven't heard from in a while. Give your best friend a call, even if you only want to say hello. Reconnect with old friends over social media, or even send an email to let someone know you're thinking of them.

With our busy lives, people sometimes need reminders to keep in touch, and air signs are the perfect ones to take that step!

Read a Book

Air signs love learning, communication, and the written word, so it makes sense that they'd also be interested in reading. If there's a book you've been dying to read or a magazine article that caught your eye, take some time for yourself and spend it reading, even if you only get to finish a couple of pages.

Not sure what you want to read? Head to your local library to check out some of the selections there. Look for a well-known classic like *Don Quixote* by Cervantes (a fellow air sign!), or try something brand-new and trendy. Still not sure where to start? Ask your librarian for a recommendation and start a conversation about some awesome books!

De-Stress with Kiteflying

_____

Sometimes, acting like a kid is a great way to release stress. And what is a better throwback activity for an air sign than flying a kite! Air signs can easily get wrapped up in their own thoughts, so an activity like flying kites that gets you out into the natural world, and gives you something to take your mind off your worries, can be a big help for your stress level. If you find you really enjoy kiteflying, you might consider checking out a kiteflying competition to develop your skills even more and make some new friends. You may even get a little exercise from chasing your kite around!

Release Sky Lanterns

Create time for yourself to take care of your spiritual needs! If you've recently experienced a loss of someone from your life, it is important to honor both those people and your own feelings. Turn to your air sign–inspired appreciation for nature and call upon the energy in the air around you for some help by releasing a fire-retardant sky lantern. (Just be sure to check regulations in your area and research the safest method and locations for releasing the lanterns before doing so.) Simply write a message on the lantern to your loved one and then release it into the sky. Allowing the air, your influencing element, to carry your message where it needs to be can give you the closure and release you've been seeking.

Accent Your Outfit
with Blue Sapphires

The rich, deep blue shade of sapphire harmonizes with Aquarius's electric nature. These precious gemstones are one of the hardest minerals on earth and can actually be several shades of blue or violet. You can find men's and women's polished sapphire jewelry, or check out raw sapphire stones, which can take on an almost iridescent hue and are most often light blue.

If you'd like to see a stunningly large and flawless blue sapphire, visit the Smithsonian National Museum of Natural History in Washington, DC, which houses the almost 423-carat Logan Sapphire, mined from Sri Lanka.

Brighten Your Space
with Torchiere Lamps

Torchiere lamps offer dramatic lighting to a space by projecting light toward the ceiling, where it is cast all around the area. Halogen torchiere options allow Aquarius to do some clear-headed thinking, reading, or relaxing in a well-lit space. If you have dark rooms in your house, consider this type of lamp to renew the space.

Look for a recently manufactured torchiere lamp with multiple brightness settings depending on the mood you want to set. (Never use a halogen bulb above 300 watts.) These lamps are available in many finishes, so they'll match with any home décor you already have.

Get Some Fresh Air

———————

Here's an easy way for air signs to take care of themselves: head outside to get some fresh air! Air signs truly value freedom and openness, so make sure to break up your day by spending some time outside. Take your morning coffee out to your porch, enjoy a book outside, or spend some time outdoors during the evenings and weekends. Choose to walk instead of drive wherever possible—not only will you feel healthier and more refreshed, but the environment will thank you as well!

"Vitamin O"—oxygen—is one of the most important factors to keep an air sign feeling revitalized and healthy.

Record Your Ideas

Air signs are creative and often have a lot of ideas. Those ideas may be interesting and worth exploring in more detail, but they can sometimes require a little more thought than you're able to give in the moment. So give yourself an outlet to brainstorm and release those ideas in a constructive manner by writing everything down and keeping a record of your ideas—no matter how big or small they seem. You may consider keeping a journal and taking some time every day to record your thoughts, or you may just want to jot down your notes on your smartphone as they come to you.

Keep an eye out for patterns in your thinking—they might help reveal worries or build on broader ideas you didn't even realize you had.

Learn about Aikido

Inspired by various martial arts techniques, aikido is more than fighting—it's really about self-development, focus, peace, and balance. Participants can use their practice to find what they need, whether that's a healthy workout or a focus on spirituality. To get started, look for beginners' classes in your area or check on online course offerings for a better idea of what to expect before signing up.

Perfect for air signs, aikido is a powerful and beautiful martial art. Since air signs may enjoy opportunities for self-improvement and collaboration, aikido can be a great way to focus your overactive mind. You'll appreciate the graceful movements that will remind you of your air-like qualities.

Perform Random Acts
of Kindness

Air signs can be extremely thoughtful; they're great at being objective when they need to be and genuinely want to see positive changes in the world around them. An easy way for air signs to help make a small change every day is to complete a random act of kindness. This can be anything from adding some extra coins to a parking meter that's about to run out to volunteering for a good cause. You could also pay for your coworker's coffee when you see them in the drive-thru line behind you, pack your partner's lunch for the day, or call an elderly relative just to chat about their week.

Making simple acts of kindness a daily ritual can strengthen your relationships by showing others how much you care about them, and can improve your own everyday outlook!

Create the Perfect Work Space

Air signs are intellectual problem-solvers with great critical-thinking skills. Make sure your work space is ready! Whether you work at home or spend your days in a professional office, it's important to make sure you create a productive work space. Start with your chair so you're comfortable and able to focus. Your chair should be lightweight and on rollers so you can move around easily. Your spontaneous nature will appreciate the ease with which you can shift around and collaborate with your coworkers.

If you work around a lot of computers and technical equipment, ask an expert about setting up a portable ionizer to help neutralize their electromagnetic vibrations. It will help improve the air quality and keep you feeling your best.

Support Clean Air

The environment is important to everyone, and air pollution is a cause any air sign can really get behind. It's important to take care of your health, and air signs will instinctually gravitate toward clean air as a way to keep their bodies strong, healthy, and happy.

Get involved in the movement for clean air! Do some research to learn about particular causes you'd like to support, like wind farms or other alternative energies. Donate to major clean air groups to help them fund their important work. Find out what programs exist in your area where you can volunteer your time. Air signs are great communicators, so volunteer your skills to help get the word out on clean air!

Invent Something!

———————

Aquarius rules all inventions and inventors, so if you have a unique idea, run with it! Many people think of interesting ideas but then don't follow through—instead, look up patents to see if anything similar has been done, then brainstorm how you can make your idea come to fruition.

Even if you just treat this idea as a hobby that you work on in your free time, it can be an exciting and motivating way to build confidence and have fun! And who knows—you might just think of the best invention since sliced bread.

Whistle Your Way
Through Chores

Vacuuming or washing dishes might not be your favorite activity, but sometimes those boring chores simply need to get done. Intellectual air signs need some kind of fun activity to keep the mind otherwise occupied, especially when faced with a few hours of dusting and sweeping. Try whistling or humming while doing chores. It'll help keep your brain focused as you work, and may be a good creative outlet if you're especially interested in music. You'll also help strengthen your lungs—all that humming is a mini-breathing exercise!

Unplug Before Bed

Even the most communicative air sign will sometimes need a break to feel refreshed and reenergized after a long day. Getting a good night's sleep will also help rejuvenate your nervous system, so do whatever you can to ensure pleasant dreams and a restful evening.

A good first step is to unplug from social media before heading to bed, and, if possible, keep technology out of the bedroom entirely. Stop scrolling through social media and give yourself a break from your tablet or computer. Minimize your information input by avoiding TV—especially news programs—before bedtime. If possible you can even eliminate clocks from your bedroom for a more peaceful sleep.

Sample Some Black Popcorn

Sure, the commercialized yellow popcorn you've seen for years is a classic snack food. But it's also boring, and Aquarius isn't boring!

Black popcorn, on the other hand, is a gourmet treat. It's made from a different type of kernel, one that is smaller and mostly disintegrates when popped. (So you get far fewer hull pieces stuck in between your teeth!) It has lots of flavor, and you can still season it with butter or oil and salt. Black popcorn (look for organic types if you prefer) is available at specialty grocery stores or online.

Take Up Tennis

Take some inspiration from fellow air sign Serena Williams, and try tennis (or racquetball)! Many air signs experience bursts of energy, which work well for a sport like tennis. It's no surprise that tennis or racquetball can be great workouts that develop muscles, improve hand-eye coordination, and strengthen heart health. But as an intellectual air sign, you might also find you enjoy the tactical nature of the game. Your critical-thinking skills might help you figure out the techniques, moves, and patterns you need to win the game. Clear your mind from other thoughts and focus on keeping your movements strong and fluid.

Wear an Ankle Bracelet

Ankle bracelets are a timeless fashion statement that can call much-deserved attention to an often-forgotten part of your body. Since Aquarius rules ankles, what better way to pay homage to your sign and show off your ankles than wearing an ankle bracelet?

You can find an ankle bracelet to match any style preference—thin and delicate, chunky and eye-catching, and everything in between. They're perfect for warm-weather wear, but don't forget about them in the colder weather—a little shine between your pants and your shoes is an unexpected delight.

Brighten Your Home with Bird-of-Paradise Flowers

When the weather is gray for an extended period of time, you might need cheering up. A surefire way to bring a smile to your face and a splash of color to your home is by filling a vase with fresh flowers.

Bird-of-paradise flowers are one especially amazing choice. These brightly colored, stunning flowers have pointed petals (they're usually yellow or orange) and incredible height and are native to South Africa. They almost resemble origami in their simple beauty. A tall, narrow vase would help showcase their shape and makes a real statement on an otherwise empty table.

Highlight Your Eyes with Glittery Eyeshadow

When you're headed out for a crazy night on the town, let your face match your excitement! No matter what your gender is, apply some glittery eyeshadow and let the music move you.

Shades of blue, purple, and green work especially well for Aquarius, so visit your favorite beauty supply store and choose a glitter shadow that matches your outfit. The light at the nightclub will catch and reflect your glittery accents and add to the party atmosphere. Your individuality will shimmer and shine through the noise—so everyone knows you're you.

Take a Pilot Training Course

_____

If air travel gets your heart racing in a good way, don't just settle for being a traveler squished into a middle seat. Put yourself in the cockpit with a pilot training course!

It's not as farfetched as it seems. Aquarius rules air travel, so it's a good match for your sign—and your desire to find your own way in life. Search online for a reputable pilot training school near you, and then ask about their introductory programs. (You'll likely get ground training and then flight training.) The adrenaline rush of soaring above the world as you pilot the plane will keep you motivated to finish the course and receive your pilot's license.

Indulge in Cardamom in Your Coffee

If your morning cup of coffee is starting to become boring, mix things up by adding a bit of cardamom to it. Cardamom has a bold, herbal flavor with hints of citrus that really boost the flavor of your morning brew. You can buy ground cardamom or whole pods at a local gourmet or natural food store.

To get the freshest flavor, grind some seeds from a single cardamom pod yourself and add the powder to the coffee grounds before you brew it. High quality cardamom can be expensive, but it's well worth a splurge every once in a while to treat yourself.

Pick Up a Foreign Language

Air signs are all about the exchange of information. It's important to them that they be able to get the word out and share their thoughts with others. Talking with new people helps you feel revitalized, so expand your communication skills by learning a foreign language. Try taking a course at your local community college or checking out one of the many apps and online programs to help you develop your skills. You may even consider planning a trip to the country that speaks that language. You'll get first-hand experience practicing your new skills and likely make new friends in the process!

Avoid Negative
Conversation Overload

Air signs are social and love to talk with other people. Since words are so important, air signs are also great at listening. But remember this: don't let yourself get burned out by tuning into negative conversations that don't involve you. Air signs can pick up other people's vibrations and energies through words, which can sometimes lead to a mental overload. Take a break and step away from the conversation, head outside for some fresh air, or redirect your focus toward something less draining and more relevant for you.

Learn to Dance

Fluid, airy movements are aesthetically pleasing to air signs, so you may enjoy watching ballet or modern dance. If you're feeling ready to jump up and start dancing yourself, consider signing up for a class to learn more about those styles. Dance has a lot of benefits for your physical health—you can develop your strength, increase your flexibility, and improve your posture. But it can also be an effective way to relieve stress and build confidence. As you focus on learning specific steps and developing your skills, you'll have the opportunity to clear your mind so you feel refreshed and ready to take on the rest of the day.

Collect Wish Dolls

Wish dolls are tiny, personalized creations that can hold your hopes and dreams and help them come true. Aquarius can appreciate all sorts of knowledge and power, and wish dolls can help the universe hear and act on your dreams.

You can make your own wish doll by wrapping a square of fabric over a large cotton ball. (The cotton ball will be the doll's head and the remaining fabric will drape down to create the body.) Then, roll a small, rectangular piece of fabric into a straight line to become the doll's arms. Use a length of yarn to wrap the two pieces together into a doll shape. Once your doll is complete, whisper a wish to it every night and sleep with it under your pillow for forty days. This magical doll might just help make your wish come true!

Listen to Mozart

———————

You've probably heard of Wolfgang Amadeus Mozart, but did you know he was also an Aquarius who followed his own path in life, choosing to be essentially a freelance musician instead of remaining a composer for a particular royal court? Inviting this fellow Aquarian's music into your life can help you feel more relaxed, centered, and connected to the universe.

Mozart was a musical genius at a very young age—he began playing public concerts before he was six. He then had a meteoric rise to fame, playing multiple instruments and eventually composing his own operas and symphonies.

Like other Aquarians, Mozart was brilliant, hardworking, and ahead of his time. Cue up his *Symphony No. 41* (also called *Jupiter*) and let the music wash over you.

Ride a Unicycle

Exercise is an important component of self-care for all signs, and Aquarius in particular is known for his excellence in athletics. Try getting your blood moving in a unique way by riding a unicycle.

Learning to ride a unicycle requires strong leg and core muscles and a commanding sense of balance—challenges that Aquarius can meet because this activity is so fun to do; it doesn't feel like work. It's also a great way to get out of an exercise funk while burning calories and taking your mind off your worries. After a few classes, you'll be proficient enough to start wowing your friends with cool tricks.

Decorate with Wind Chimes

Air signs can sometimes have the energy of a powerful wind with their free-spirited natures. Why not bring that inspiration into your home décor? Try putting some wind chimes on your porch, by the entrance to your home, or somewhere else where you'll be able to hear them often. If you live in an apartment, putting your chimes near a window should be enough to get them ringing.

Putting a wind chime in your home can be a great way to remind yourself of some of your great air sign qualities. Every time you hear it ringing, you'll be reminded of your fun, adventurous side!

Become a Social Butterfly

Connection is your strong suit, so head out to events, get-togethers, and parties to meet new people. Social events bring out the best in air signs, who are in their element when surrounded by engaging conversation and interesting ideas. Try attending a reading at your local bookstore, checking out the speakers at a nearby college, or simply following your friends to a party. Socializing with different types of people comes naturally to air signs, so you may find your friend group growing rapidly in ways you never expected. You'll increase your own knowledge of the world by meeting other people, so don't be afraid to let your natural social butterfly tendencies shine!

Go See Neon Light Art

Neon lights are best known for announcing whether a store or restaurant is open or closed, but they can also become amazing works of art too. Whether shaped into recognizable objects like lips or words, or arranged into cool patterns, neon light art is a stylish, innovative take on modern art.

Your local art museum might have a visiting exhibit of neon light art, or you might want to take a trip to a large city to see some. Wandering around checking out the unique colors and shapes will open your mind to the myriad ways to see and enjoy art around you every day.

Put a Penguin Stuffed Animal on Your Bed

————————————

Stuffed animals aren't just for kids anymore! Put a cute plush penguin on your bed to make you smile and laugh every time you see it. Penguins are ruled by Uranus, Aquarius' ruling planet, and are a perfect example of individual ingenuity in service of the collective—they often huddle together in large groups to stay warm.

Look for a stuffed penguin at your local toy store, or purchase one from a charity that is working to protect their habitat. To spread the love, buy a second one and donate it to a children's charity in your area or give it to a child you know.

Sign Up for a Writing Course

Air signs are known for being great at expression and deep thinking. So why not expand your communication skills by taking a writing course? Although it may seem intimidating to put all your thoughts onto paper, you may be surprised to find you have a hidden writing talent! The good news is, writing classes span a variety of areas from fiction and poetry to screenwriting and presentation development. You're sure to find something that fits your interests!

You may find that you thrive in a social environment, like a class at a local college, where you can share your ideas with your classmates and develop your skills together. But if you're feeling a little shy about sharing your first writing attempts in person, there are plenty of online courses you can explore to get started.

Become Inspired by Lightning

Your Aquarian mind works like lightning—offering powerful bolts of amazing ideas, innovative theories, and sparkling creativity. Remind yourself of your infinite potential for greatness by adorning your work area with an image of a lightning bolt.

You can look for a sculpture-like lightning bolt decoration, a stunning nature photograph of real lightning, or a neon light lightning bolt if you're feeling adventurous. Every time you glance at the lightning, you'll be motivated to come up with your next brilliant idea.

Grow Hydroponic Vegetables

Taking good care of your body starts by being mindful of what you put in it. Organic and freshly grown vegetables are the foundation of a healthy diet. Try growing your own vegetables at home in an environmentally friendly way—hydroponically.

Hydroponic gardening is the process of growing food with no soil. This method produces high-quality food, takes up less space than soil-based gardens, and is easy to set up in urban or small settings. To get started, do a lot of research on what is involved, and ask your local nursery or other experts for resources for growing your own hydroponic vegetables. Leafy greens are typically an easy crop for beginners to try.

Watch a Science Fiction Movie

There's something exciting and a little scary about space and science fiction movies—they push your imagination to the limit and encourage you to ponder all the possibilities of the universe.

All astronaut, science fiction, and space movies are Aquarian-ruled, so make some snacks and settle in to watch a movie in this genre. Whether you opt for time-honored classics like *Alien* or *2001: A Space Odyssey* or a new thriller like *Interstellar* or *The Martian*, you'll find yourself thinking about the plot long after the ending credits. Aquarius likes to let his imagination run wild, and these types of movies will help you do just that.

Head to the Swimming Pool

It may come as a surprise, but swimming is actually great for air signs. Air signs are known for loving to think about problems from every angle, but sometimes it's important to have a mental break. With swimming you'll need to focus on mastering each movement and maintaining fluid motions, so it's a great way to calm your mind. Allow yourself to relax and feel restored as you take a break from your worries.

Swimming is also a great way for air signs to get some exercise. Regular swim sessions will help you build lung power and stamina. So instead of your regular workout, head to your local pool and do some laps.

Keep Communication Open

E ven great communicators like air signs can have disagreements with friends and family members. But you're likely to feel unbalanced when conflict causes the lines of communication to be closed. So clear the air and reopen those lines. It's important to remember not to hold onto grudges, so if you have any negative feelings, try to let them go and approach the conversation with a positive attitude. Do your best to be patient and flexible with the other person—remember, not everyone is as good at expression as you are! Work together to get back in balance and bring your relationships to a happier state.

Tap Into the Power
of Lapis Lazuli

Crystals and gemstones have the power to help you fulfill your dreams and restore your inner balance. Lapis lazuli is a brilliant blue stone that's especially effective for Aquarius. It's known to help you discover your purpose and live whatever dreams your imagination thinks up.

Carry a piece of lapis lazuli in your left pocket (you receive energy through your left side and release it through your right), or place a chunk of it on your desk at work. Whenever you touch or see it, you'll be reminded of the astounding abilities you were born to showcase.

Listen to Electronic Music

Traditional instruments offer beautiful sounds, but electronic options really kick music up a notch energy-wise. The unusual and unexpected notes and sounds you hear in electronic music keep you guessing—and dancing.

Look online for electronic music that speaks to you, or visit a local club to listen to some live. Or—even better—pop into a recording studio or get some software, so you can compose your own electronic song! Whether it has a percussive base or a cool remix patched in, you'll find yourself moving to the beat of your own sound.

Fight Seasonal Blues with Light

I n cold weather months the lack of strong sunlight (or any sunlight!) can start to wear on you after a while. If you can't swing a trip to a tropical spot, bring light right into your home with a high-quality light box.

Check with your doctor to make sure a light box is a good match for your health profile, and then research brands and cost to find one that fits your needs. Ask your doctor when is the most beneficial time to use it and for how long. The infusion of light might help recharge your batteries and get you ready to tackle your day.

Hang Up a Photo of Your Planet

Your ruling planet of Uranus is stunningly beautiful. This gas giant, which resides about two billion miles away from the sun, spins on its side, and is a lovely blue color (thanks to the methane gas in its upper atmosphere, which reflects blue light).

Hanging a photo of your planet near where you work will inspire you to follow your own path—just as Uranus spins in a different direction than any other planet in our solar system. It will also remind you to persevere in difficult times, since Uranus spins that way because of a series of collisions with a huge object billions of years ago. The planet withstood the blows and carried on, spinning in its own unique way.

Attend an Interesting Lecture

Air signs are naturally curious and love learning, so try attending a lecture or other form of presentation. Keep it fun and interesting by attending lectures on subjects that pique your curiosity. You may even be able to find presentations by popular speakers for free through your local library or other organizations in your area. Take some time for yourself to learn something new!

Doing something mentally stimulating will put all air signs in a good mood, but attending a lecture can also have an added social benefit. You may find yourself making friends with your fellow attendees as you discuss your shared interests after the event is over.

Display Blue Cornflowers
in the Summer

Cornflowers, which are native to Europe but now found in many places in North America, come in a brilliant blue shade that is Aquarius's color. They sometimes grow like weeds, so take a walk around your neighborhood and see if you can gather any. (If not, consider cultivating cornflowers yourself—they germinate quickly and are easy to grow.)

Display a bunch of cornflowers in a simple vase that lets the flowers shine. They don't last long after you cut them, so enjoy their cheerful color while you can!

Bring Back Ragtime Music

———————————

Ragtime's unmistakable syncopated rhythm is infectious and joyful. Though ragtime isn't one of the most popular music styles out there today, don't let that stop you from enjoying it. Search online for a classic ragtime composition, like Scott Joplin's (the King of Ragtime) "Maple Leaf Rag," or look for more modern acts that feature ragtime, like Bob Milne. The beat will soon have you bouncing around, forgetting your worries, and savoring the unique sounds.

Enjoy a Rainy Day

Air signs are connected to the weather—after all, your mood can change just as quickly and drastically as the winds! Take some time to connect with and appreciate changes in the weather instead of letting them get you down. Don't let yourself get upset by a rainy day. Instead, enjoy a good rainstorm! Sit by your window and simply savor the wind and rain. You may find it helps you relax to bring a cup of tea with you or take a few deep, meditative breaths. By training yourself to look at things in a positive light, you'll take better care of your emotional needs and feel happier every day.

Balance Your Mind
and Body with Pilates

———————————

E ven though air signs are often focused on the
mind, it's just as important to take care of the
body through exercise. The secret to consistent
exercise? Find a workout routine that works for
you and that you enjoy! Not only will your body feel
healthy and strong, but you'll also head into your
workout with a much more positive attitude.

One routine that might work well for air signs is a
Pilates class, which focuses on both the mind and the
body as you work your way through different moves.
You'll learn to strengthen your physique through
careful movement, develop your flexibility and
balance, and properly manage your breathing for
less stress and more control of your body.

Hang Up an
Octagon-Shaped Mirror

This type of mirror is as unique as you—what a perfect décor item for Aquarius. Hang an octagon-shaped mirror by your door so you can check your look before you head out. Arrange it over a small table or shelf that can hold your keys, mail, and other essentials, and you've got a useful and distinctive entryway design. The mirror's unusual shape will also surprise your guests and encourage them to check it—and themselves—out.

Invest in a Home Weather Station

The winds on Aquarius-ruled planet Uranus can be quite formidable, blowing at up to about 500 mph. Though we thankfully don't experience that sort of extreme weather on earth, we do see our share of interesting storms and forces of nature—both of which probably pique your curiosity.

Consider buying a high-tech, Wi-Fi–enabled home weather station so you can keep track of weather patterns (like temperature, rain amounts, and humidity) and stay abreast of potentially dangerous storms in your area.

If you live in the country, try to watch storms from a safe place where you can take in the vast horizon. If you live in the city and it's safe, head to a skyscraper to view interesting weather rolling in. Let the awesome power of nature remind you of your place in our infinite universe.

Watch the News
(at the Right Time)

Today's constant 24/7 news cycle means that there's an immense amount of information available out there. Watching or reading the news keeps you informed about current events, geopolitical situations, and local goings-on, and your creative mind might even be sparked by patterns you see in news stories. For example, you could recognize trends in fashion, real estate, or food, and apply them to your line of work.

There is a caveat though: monitor your news intake before bedtime. Inevitably, you'll see upsetting stories that could affect your sleep, and Aquarius already struggles with insomnia at times. Instead, follow a relaxing, calming bedtime routine, and save your intake of news for other times of the day.

Experiment with Calligraphy

If you're an air sign, you're all about communication. Get creative with your communication style and study calligraphy! Calligraphy is a beautiful writing form that can take a lot of practice to master but can also be a rewarding skill. You may be able to share your abilities for things like wedding invitations, announcements, or memorials.

Calligraphy can also be a meditative practice, giving overthinking air signs a much-needed mental break. Allow yourself time to slow down and focus on each careful, deliberate movement instead of worrying about a problem at hand. Taking a break to focus on your calligraphy will help you redirect your attention and feel refreshed.

Have a Good Laugh

Social air signs love to have a good time with their friends and family. Look for ways you can enjoy a laugh together! While the emotional and social benefits of sharing a laugh are clear, did you know laughter can also help your physical health by decreasing stress, lowering blood pressure, relieving pain, and even boosting your immune system? Taking some time to laugh every day will have a wide range of restorative benefits.

All you need to do is head to a comedy club or watch a silly movie. Or keep a book of puns, jokes, and limericks handy for when you need a pick me-up or a reason to share a giggle with other people. Your love of language will make it doubly enjoyable for you!

Relax with a Blue Ice Cocktail

Since blue is Aquarius's color, this fun cocktail is a perfect way to unwind after a busy week. Add 1 shot vodka, 1 shot blue curaçao, 3 ounces soda (such as Sprite), and a large handful of ice cubes to a blender. Combine until slushy and serve in a martini glass. The electric blue color of the curaçao will make you feel like you're on a warm beach somewhere. Close your eyes and hear the sound of the waves crashing and feel the sand in your toes.

Invest in an Air Purifier

As an air sign, you know that the quality of the air around you is important for your health and well-being. Clean air is especially important for your physical health if you have asthma or other lung issues, but the truth is that everyone can benefit! Keeping dust, smog, and other tiny particles out of your lungs is an important way to not only keep you feeling your best, but also helps prevent other illnesses. Research and invest in a good air purifier to help eliminate things like pollen, smoke, or other pollutants from the air in your home. An air purifier can be especially important if you live in a city where the increased population and traffic can mean more pollution.

Be Grateful for Good Friendships

Reflecting on good friendships you have is a great way to show gratitude and appreciation for the role they play in your life. It's easy to get busy and accidentally take friendships for granted, so take a few moments to really think about yours.

Try a concentration exercise: as you sit comfortably and breathe slowly and deeply, contemplate how grateful you are for your friendships. Whether it's a longtime friendship that dates back to your childhood or a new friend you just met at work, these connections make you happy, keep you entertained, and offer support at difficult times. Friendships bring out the best in humanity, and reminding yourself of that is a wonderful way to see all the good in the world.

Wear Clothes with Patterns

Aquarius tends to be passionately individual, and your clothes should reflect your personality. Take a look at your closet and drawers, and make sure you have plenty of outfits with patterns and style. A periwinkle blue gingham checked shirt, a scarf with neon zigzags, colored pinstriped pants, a sheer skirt with metallic thread to wear over leggings—no design is off-limits for Aquarius, and the brighter the colors, the better. Update your clothes periodically, and visit thrift stores or consignment shops for great deals on pieces that are unique and one of a kind—just like you!

Don't Get Stuck in Ruts

If you're starting to feel like you live in that movie *Groundhog Day*—seeing the same people all the time; wearing the same boring, black outfit; eating the same dinners every week—it's time to shake things up. Your world is expansive and diverse, and Aquarius needs to follow his own path and keep things fresh. Reinvigorate yourself in body, mind, and spirit by meeting up with a new crowd, showcasing a new outfit, or trying a new recipe. Then set a monthly reminder on your phone to check in with yourself to see if you need to break out of another rut.

Unwind with
Frankincense and Myrrh

Most people only know frankincense and myrrh as two of the gifts the Three Wise Men brought to baby Jesus after he was born. But they are also powerful essential oils that you can burn as incense to create a special atmosphere in your home. Myrrh is known to promote spirituality, heal wounds (which is why it's found in some skin creams), and boost the immune system. Frankincense has a warm, woodsy scent and can soothe anxiety, minimize insomnia, and improve memory.

The combination creates a calming atmosphere for meditation or just to help you transition from a busy day to bedtime. You can look for incense sticks at your local health or New Age store or online.

Create a Bright, Open Home

A ir signs are always on the move and can seem a little restless. So it's important that you use your home space as a place to restore and refocus. Create a beautiful, air-friendly home where you'll feel comfortable and able to relax.

Your design aesthetic is likely to be light, open, and airy. To start, don't set up your living spaces with so many components that they feel overcomplicated— simple spaces are important to air signs! Also, take some time to think about the lighting for your home. All the lights in your home should be full spectrum, which will help imitate the sunny outdoors, even on the rainiest days.

Listen to Raga Music

Raga is a classical musical custom that origi-nated in India to create a peaceful mood. Its name comes from the Sanskrit word *raga*, which means "color" or "to color," implying that the music colors the feelings or disposition of the audience. There are many types of raga, ranging from shorter pieces like songs to lengthier, more involved pieces that can incorporate a musician's improvisation. Look online for various raga music until you find a style that speaks to you. Then play it when you want some quiet, reflective time for yourself.

Give Your Car a Makeover

———————

Say the word *Aquarius*, and people are likely to quote the famous "Aquarius/Let the Sunshine In" song by the band The 5th Dimension. But the other lyrics in that song are just as important—they describe a world where everyone lives in harmony and is guided by love above all else. Show your allegiance to the Age of Aquarius by decorating your car with psychedelic stripes or designs, so everyone will know you are a hippie at heart—meaning, one who appreciates and respects all kinds of people, cultures, and lifestyles.

Play the Bells

A gorgeous set of silver bells featuring different tones can clear your space of unwanted or negative energy. Plus, their pure sound and decorative appeal make them a great addition to any home. Look in antique or music stores for bells, and be sure to play them before you purchase. You want a bell with an inviting, vibrant sound, not a piercing one.

If your home feels stifling, tense, or unsettled, ring one of the bells several times in each room. The vibration of the bell will renew and refresh your home's energy—and you get to enjoy the lovely sounds.

Hang Multicolored Mobiles

When a gentle breeze blows, allow your body, mind, and spirit to be renewed by not only the fresh air but also the lazy motion of a mobile. A double-helix shape works perfectly for this avant garde sign. Hang it on your front porch or near a window that's often open to get maximum benefit.

Look for mobiles that are brightly colored and visually interesting, so they're especially fascinating to look at. Don't forget to share the joy with the little ones in your life, too—hang a mobile securely and safely out of their reach and let kids sit under it and experience the whimsical entertainment.

Chill Out with Some Popular Music

E xploring new sounds and music styles is important, but it's also perfectly fine to enjoy songs
that are well known. Artists who are true to themselves, unique, and energetic are good fits for
Aquarius. In particular, Justin Timberlake, Shakira,
Alicia Keys, and Adam Lambert offer songs you can
dance to, both for exercise and to take your mind off
your day. The reggae beat of Bob Marley classics is
fun for a change of pace. If you're in the mood for
upbeat country, throw on some of Garth Brooks's
rollicking favorites. If you'd rather hear some glam
rock, turn on the inimitable Alice Cooper.

Photograph a Flock of Migrating Birds

Aquarius rules group efforts, and what better natural display of a group effort than a majestic flock of migrating birds? Each bird knows their role and plays a part in the greater good. They stay together and help each other get to their destination. Witnessing this amazing skill is a humbling sight indeed. Capture the moment forever by taking high-quality photos of the flock.

Find a spot that's comfortable while you wait for them to go by, and remain unobtrusive to other plants and animals around you. When the time is right, snap the pictures and later hang a large version of one in your home to remind you of your ability to help your group (be it family, work, or another type) get where it needs to go.

Perform a Marionette Show for Kids

Puppet shows are a perennial favorite for children (and adults)—the quirky characters, the funny dialogue, and the simple sets lend themselves to an unforgettable show. Purchase or create some puppets and then think of a few short stories to tell with them. The stories don't need to be intricate—the props themselves are a big part of the show! Express your unique creativity through the puppets' tales of rousing mischief, sidesplitting tomfoolery, sensational victories, and hilarious failures. Create silly voices for each, and then find some young audience members to delight with this old-fashioned entertainment.

Think Through Your Decisions

A ir signs are great at critical thinking and like to make logical decisions. They'd rather follow their heads than let their emotions get in the way of their decision-making. Yet, because air signs like to take their time to see all sides of a question, making big decisions can prove difficult.

The best advice here is to not let yourself get rushed or pressured into making a decision. If you're feeling unbalanced, you can get trapped thinking in and out of hundreds of potential scenarios—many of which will never occur! If this happens, remember to take care of your emotions and your body; try doing some deep breathing and allowing your intuition to help you figure out which solutions are the best for you.

Take Care of Yourself

If you're an air sign, you know you can sometimes get trapped in your own head. Air signs are intellectual people, which makes them great problem-solvers and critical thinkers. However, there's always the risk of overthinking and spending too much time living in your mind. Don't let yourself get too detached from daily life!

Completing necessary, practical activities is essential self-care. Things like eating three good meals a day, showering, and brushing your teeth every morning and evening are important for keeping your life in balance. So remember to stay grounded in the real world and do the things you need to do to keep yourself healthy and happy.

Try Feng Shui

It's important to get a good night's sleep so you wake up feeling enlivened and reinvigorated. For air signs, sleep is also an important aspect of keeping your nervous system in balance. Use the power of some basic feng shui to help you get exactly the right setup for better rest.

Feng shui is the practice of aligning and arranging elements in your home to create the ideal energy flow for positivity and good luck in various aspects of your life. To improve sleep, you should avoid positioning the bed so your feet point toward the bedroom door, which can decrease your personal energy. Considering things like the way other furniture in your bedroom can impede the flow of energy can also be helpful to improve your sleep.

Breathe Deeply

Air signs have highly tuned nervous systems, so certain breathing exercises can help you stay calm and relaxed. For a simple breathing technique you can employ anywhere, start by counting up from one to ten on an exhale. Then try counting down from ten to one as you inhale. You may find it helpful to close your eyes or put your hands on your stomach or chest to feel yourself breathing. Check out online resources or apps for alternate techniques. Whenever you're feeling a little stressed, take a moment to focus on yourself and your breathing.

Consider a Pet Bird

Dogs and cats are favorite domestic pets, but a bird might be a better fit for your Aquarian personality. In particular, mynahs and cockatoos are spirited, intelligent birds that can learn to speak. These types of birds can be wonderful companions and will help keep a smile on your face and love in your heart. You may find that you buoy each other's mood and look forward to seeing each other. Cockatoos are even known to dance—join in the fun and dance along with yours! If you've never had a pet bird before, it is best to start small, perhaps a parakeet. Just make sure to get expert advice on adopting (and properly caring for) your chosen bird from a local animal shelter before you commit.

Incorporate Turmeric Into Your Diet

Turmeric is an earthy, ginger-like spice that might have the power to help reduce inflammation, lower cholesterol levels, ease headaches, and alleviate symptoms of depression and arthritis. Plus, it's easy to consume: blend it into a smoothie, sprinkle it on roasted vegetables, or whip up a curry recipe that uses turmeric.

This bold orange spice is a healthy addition to any diet. If you're just getting started with turmeric, try simply sprinkling some on meat before you roast it. The warm taste of the turmeric will add a comforting dimension to the dish.

Play a Kazoo

Aquarius is an air sign—which means proper breathing is especially important to your health and well-being. Practicing slow, deep breaths through meditation is one great way to reduce stress and renew your energy levels, but another—louder and perhaps more fun way—is to play the kazoo.

That's right—the silly kids' toy is a great relaxation tool for you too. Whether you just make sounds or try to play an actual song, the kazoo can help Aquarius consciously exhale and let go of worries. Whistle a familiar tune or just see how loud you can make the sounds—you'll soon realize you're laughing and have forgotten about your cares.

Relax with Cedarwood
Essential Oil

E ssential oils are versatile healing agents that can help restore your overall well-being either through aromatherapy or diluted topical use. Cedarwood in particular is helpful for Aquarius, because it can relieve tense muscles, stimulate circulation, and soothe the mind. You can add a drop of the oil (diluted according to instructions) to your regular moisturizer for topical use or use it in aromatherapy, perhaps diffused with reeds. Let its calming effects relax you as you imagine the majestic Himalayan forests filled with the evergreen trees that produce this oil.

Plant Blue Hydrangeas

If you're looking for a large, flowering bush to fill out a garden or walkway, look no further than the beautiful blue hydrangea. Its giant flowers are stunning to behold and add unique color to a garden. Ask your local nursery which varieties would grow well in your area, as well as soil recommendations for how to keep the flowers looking blue, and then get planting. The fullness of the flowers does a lovely job of filling a low vase, so be sure to cut a bunch to brighten the inside of your home as well.

Listen to Old Radio Programs

Aquarius rules the Internet...and also its older equivalent, the radio! Take a break from today's loud, graphic-filled media and relax with only the sounds of radio programs filling the air. Take a few minutes to read about how the radio was invented and became popular, and then find recordings of a few old radio shows that pique your interest. Whether it's a mystery hour, comedy routine, or variety show, listen to the whole program and imagine yourself living in simpler times several generations ago.

Decorate with Clear Quartz

Crystals can be a great way to add some beauty to a space and help rebalance your energy. Air signs will find lots of benefits from clear quartz crystals, which are among the most common and well-known healing stones. Learn about ways quartz may help treat you physically (crystal healing with clear quartz can be useful for the nervous system!) and mentally. Since clear quartz is believed to increase spiritual connections and clear thinking, it can be a useful tool when you need to expand your thoughts and think carefully.

Try decorating your home and office space with clear quartz crystal clusters so there's always one nearby when you start to feel a little off-balance.

Choose Light, Fresh Scents

A ir signs find it helpful for their living spaces to be well lit and spacious to mimic the natural world. So it makes sense that you'd also prefer lighter, more natural scents for your home. Whether you're looking for candles, room sprays, or other scented products, choose light scents like lemon verbena and rosewater. Even if you typically hate perfumes or colognes, these scents aren't overpowering. Instead, they'll make the air smell fresh and clean, which will help you feel more relaxed and at home in your living space. Certain scents also come with plenty of other benefits—for instance, a citrusy smell can help you feel a bit more energized!

About the Author

Constance Stellas is an astrologer of Greek heritage with more than twenty-five years of experience. She primarily practices in New York City and counsels a variety of clients, including business CEOs, artists, and scholars. She has been interviewed by *The New York Times*, *Marie Claire*, and *Working Woman*, and had appeared on several New York TV morning shows, featuring regularly on Sirius XM and other national radio programs as well. Constance is the astrologer for *HuffPost* and a regular contributor to Thrive Global. She is also the author of several titles, including *The Astrology Gift Guide*, *Advanced Astrology for Life*, *The Everything® Sex Signs Book*, and the graphic novel series Tree of Keys, as well as coauthor of *The Hidden Power of Everyday Things*. Learn more about Constance at her website, ConstanceStellas.com, or on *Twitter* (@Stellastarguide).